Walks on the High

# Blencathra, Skiddaw and Borrowdale

by
Tom Bowker

Dalesman Books
1989

# Key to Maps

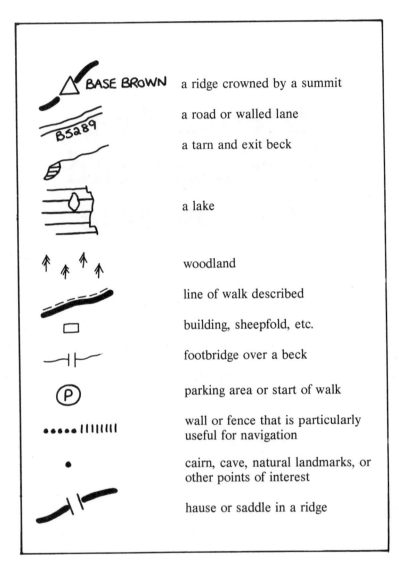

BASE BROWN — a ridge crowned by a summit

B5289 — a road or walled lane

a tarn and exit beck

a lake

woodland

line of walk described

building, sheepfold, etc.

footbridge over a beck

(P) parking area or start of walk

wall or fence that is particularly useful for navigation

cairn, cave, natural landmarks, or other points of interest

hause or saddle in a ridge

Printed by Swannack, Brown & Co., Ltd., Hull, England.

# Contents

**INTRODUCTION**

**BLENCATHRA AND BACK O'SKIDDAW**

Walk 1.   The Blencathra Classic ..................... 6

Walk 2.   Blencathra, Bannerdale Crags, Bowscale Fell and  9
Bowscale Tarn ...........................

Walk 3.   Five Blencathra Ridges.  11

Walk 4.   Bannerdale Crags (North-East Ridge), Blencathra  14
and Souther Fell ...........................

Walk 5.   Back O'Skiddaw ...........................  15

Walk 6.   A Caldew Round .........................  19

**SKIDDAW**

Walk 7.   Skiddaw via Longside Edge .................  21

Walk 8.   Skiddaw via Skiddaw House ................  23

**BORROWDALE**

Walk 9.   High Raise and Ullscarf via Eagle Crag ........  26

Walk 10.  Bessyboot, Glaramara and Allen Crags ........  29

Walk 11.  A Borrowdale Walkabout ....................  33

Walk 12.  Dalehead via Castle Crag and High Spy .......  38

Walk 13.  The Gable Traverse ........................  41

Walk 14.  Scafell Pike via the Corridor Route ............  45

*Cover Map by Barbara Yates*
*Sketch Maps by Tom Bowker*

The Dalesman Publishing Company Ltd.
Clapham, via Lancaster, LA2 8EB.

First Published 1989

© Tom Bowker 1989

ISBN: 0 85206 962 6

# Introduction

THIS second book in a series offers walks on Blencathra, Skiddaw and their surrounding fells, and also on the high fells overlooking the head of Borrowdale. As a guidebook writer I feel myself torn between an eagerness to introduce readers to my beloved Lakeland fells, a natural desire that my books will sell, and a concern that I must accept some blame for the consequent erosion of mountain paths. With the latter in mind I try to diverge from the mountain 'motorways', thus hoping to spread the load a little.

The walks described should be treated with due respect. Boots should be worn and rucksacks should contain waterproofs, spare clothing, map, compass, whistle and survival bag. In winter a torch, balaclava, mittens and some extra food should be added. When snow and ice coat the fells an ice-axe should be carried. Crampons are becoming more commonly used by fellwalkers, and rightly so. Frequent practice in the use of map and compass make that winter day when their use suddenly becomes vital much less terrifying. Remember the cardinal rule – start using your compass from a point where you know where you are, don't wait until you are lost. Successful navigation through deteriorating conditions adds a bonus to your day and a boost to your confidence. Remember, in an emergency, all becks flow downhill and if followed with care can be fast escape routes in bad weather. Never be afraid to turn back. The fells will still be there next weekend.

Alongside each walk is a sketch map to be used in conjunction with the text. It is advisable, however, also to carry the relevant sheet of the 1:25000 The English Lakes Outdoor Leisure Maps. All the place names in the text refer to the 1982 edition of these maps. The mileages and heights of ascent are approximate and 'left' or 'right' refers to a physical feature as if facing it. Parking details are as per the maps, local authorities and tradition up to press, but are always liable to change. Limited space means I have to choose between detailed route descriptions, incidental information, and detailed descriptions of views. I tend to be niggardly with the latter, feeling it's useful for walkers to attempt to orientate the view to their map.

The only way to learn about the fells is to be out regularly in all conditions. There will be times when you are frightened and times when you are physically exhausted. Ironically, these are the days that live most vividly in the memory and when you learn something about the mountains. Don't forget that it's a game, it's fun, it's adventure. For the fellwalker, given reasonable fitness and equipment, using his/her commonsense, the dangers are more apparent than real. Statistically, you are probably in more danger in your home or on your journey to and from the fells.

The Lakeland fells have become inextricably woven into the weft of my life. My addiction to climbing them led to love, marriage and fatherhood, and innumerable friendships. They stimulated my interest in writing and are the bedrock of its continuing development. They have given me untold days of rewarding physical endeavour, good company, and wonderment at the beauty seen. If this booklet should bring such pleasures to any who read it I will be content. Happy walking!

**Tom Bowker**

January 1989

# BLENCATHRA AND BACK O'SKIDDAW

**Walk 1**

**6 miles**
**2300 feet of ascent**

## The Blencathra Classic

*Blencathra is a lovely name for a magnificent mountain. The name has Celtic roots and has been translated as 'Peak of Devils'. There's nothing devilish about this shapely beauty, however. She offers her worshippers nothing but adventure, fun, and spellbinding views over the glorious bumpy patchwork of Lakeland. In his book 'Hamish's Groats End Walk' Hamish Brown, one of Britain's most famous mountain walkers, offered to swap Blencathra for a handful of 'munros'. Praise indeed from a Scot, and an indication of the mountain's quality. The walk-cum-scramble described is the classic traverse of the fell's two finest ridges – a must for first-comers.*

*Parking/Start: On the A66 Penrith-Keswick, either in a layby on the south side of the road opposite the hamlet of Scales, or a layby on the north side of the road about half a mile nearer Keswick. (GR344269/ 339267).*

ABOUT halfway between these laybys, leave the road by a path climbing between a red-porched cottage and a farm to a gate. Beyond the gate turn right on to a path slanting up the fellside. This eventually steepens leftwards, then skirts around the rocky rim of the deep bowl of Mousthwaite Comb, before swinging left across the north-east flank of Scales Fell and descending slightly to join a path overlooking the River Glenderamackin, a gob-stopper of a name which apparently has Celtic roots. Place names indicate a long survival of British influence in north-eastern lakeland, supporting the theory that the iron

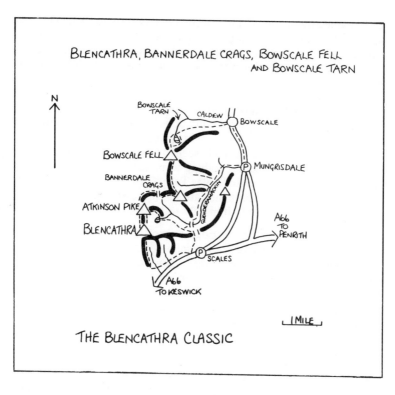

BLENCATHRA, BANNERDALE CRAGS, BOWSCALE FELL AND BOWSCALE TARN

THE BLENCATHRA CLASSIC

age fort crowning Carrock Fell (see Walk 5) was the centre of local resistance to the Roman invaders.

From this point, with luck, you will get your first glimpse of Sharp Edge. First-sighters will undoubtedly be filled with a sense of anticipation, or apprehension, or a mixture of both. Foule Crag and the steep mountain corner which Sharp Edge abuts dramatically chop off the northern end of Blencathra's summit tableland. Below these craggy defences the airy castellations of Sharp Edge are outlined by sun, hopefully. From the rims of the Edge and tableland slabby buttresses, scree fans and dank gullies spill down into the shadowy hollow cupping Scales Tarn.

Follow the path across the fellside to where Scales Beck spills down to join the Glenderamackin. Now climb the path alongside this beck to emerge on to the shore of sombre, but lovely, Scales Tarn. One day last summer I sat with a group of friends basking in the warm sunlight flooding this high combe. Sitting nearby were members of the Milton Club, courageous blind mountain walkers who were climbing Blencathra aided by canine and human helpers. Our sightless neighbours appeared to be equally enjoying the balm offered by the warm sunlight, the constant susurration of cascading water, and the excited shouts floating faintly down from the sun-kissed pinnacles of Sharp Edge.

Climb right from the tarn on to the crest of Sharp Edge. Unless you find it too scary, or ice or snow conditions forcibly prevent it, attempt to keep to the crest all the way. This gives the excitement, fun and satisfaction that is the point of an ascent by this route. If you find it too scary, however, and there's nothing to be ashamed of in admitting that, my advice is to return to Scales Tarn. Cross Scales Beck where it spills from the tarn and climb the path slanting up the grassy fellside to the south of the tarn, and ultimately to the top of Blencathra.

The excitements of Sharp Edge do not last long unfortunately. Some might think otherwise, especially whilst grappling with them. The fun does not end with the 'edge', however, for the exit slope is a steep mix of polished groove, slaty rib and scree runnel before you emerge triumphantly on to the fell rim. Under hard winter conditions Sharp Edge is no place for the inexperienced or ill-equipped. Then, an ice-axe should be carried and possibly the use of crampons, or a rope, might be called for. In winter, treat this ridge with the respect it deserves.

A path now leads along the rim of the fell overlooking Scales Tarn towards the summit. Ignore this, however, and walk west to the cairn crowning Atkinson Pike, 2772 feet, Blencathra's northern summit.

A broad grassy ridge with a dip in the middle divides the fell's north and south summits, forming the 'saddle' so obvious from the east, giving the mountain its now out of favour name of Saddleback. Head south into the dip, passing close to a small tarn and a large cross of quartz stones constructed by Harold Robinson, a Threlkeld man, to what purpose no one seems sure, but any task which involves many ascents of Blencathra has purpose enough. Climb the far slope and step up to the summit cairn of Blencathra, 2847 feet. Below your toecaps now spiny ridges cleave down gulfs of mountain air on to the rooftops of Threlkeld. Beyond, shadowy lakes glimmer and fields and fells pile up to the far blue mountains of Lakeland.

The Hall's Fell ridge starts virtually from the cairn. A rocky ridge gradually steepens south-south-easterly before twisting left then right over a section surmounted by rocky tors known as Narrow Edge. A path, however, threads around all the difficulties and given dry conditions I bet you could climb up or down this ridge with your hands in your pockets, something I wouldn't recommend on Sharp Edge. Again, however, the point in Lakeland scrambling, compared to scrambling in the Alps or Skye, is to seek out the difficulties rather than to avoid them, good conditions prevailing of course, so do attempt to stick to the crest as much as possible. Again, in winter conditions, care and the right equipment should be taken. South-facing and more amenable Hall's Fell, however, is unlikely to be quite as serious an undertaking as Sharp Edge might be. Below Narrow Edge the ridge broadens, the rocks submerge, and steep zig-zags lead down to the weir over which spills the Gate Gill beck.

Do not cross the weir. Turn left and follow a path alongside a wall to reach and cross Doddick Gill to a gate. Continue beyond to a further gate. Beyond this climb slightly left, then alongside a wall, to cross the slabby banks of Scaley Beck. Shortly beyond rejoin your outward route at a gate.

**Walk 2**

**9 miles**
**2600 feet of ascent**

# Blencathra, Bannerdale Crags, Bowscale Fell and Bowscale Tarn

*A pleasant walk of great variety, the airy thrills of Sharp Edge giving way to the amiable 'bagging' of two uncrowded two thousand footers. Bowscale Tarn is one of the Lakeland's less publicised tarns, but none the worse for this. Cupped in a surprisingly rugged combe, it's a splendid spot for a sunbathe, swim, or impromptu picnic. The Ordnance Survey, Landranger Series, Sheet 90, 1:50000, Penrith, Keswick, and Ambleside map may be useful for this walk.*

*Parking/Start: Mungrisdale. On the left, near a wooden footbridge over the river, as you enter from the A66, or in the cul-de-sac by the telephone kiosk. (GR364304).*

WALK past the telephone kiosk to a gate leading on to a path alongside the River Glenderamackin. The dominant conical peak ahead is The Tongue, a spur of Bowscale Fell. The slaty buttresses of Bannerdale Crags, rising out of the high combe of Bannerdale, come into view as you go, with the north east ridge looking particularly 'interesting'. The path curves left across a tributary beck. Ignore the rough track climbing right into Bannerdale and bear left along a fainter and swampy path clinging to the river bank.

The path shortly crosses the Bannerdale Beck before winding pleasantly, though occasionally swampily, up the ravine of the Glenderamackin. When it begins to curve right, around the base of the south east spur of Bannerdale Crags, curiously named White Horse Bent, look for a path forking left down to a footbridge over the river. Go down and cross the bridge but ignore the path climbing left from it. Instead, climb diagonally right up steep grass to join a higher crossing path. As you climb you will get your first glimpse of Sharp Edge at the head of the valley, a grey blade of rock leaning against the high corner of a rugged table mountain. It's a sudden and dramatic sighting that excites even it you've seen it many times before.

Turn right along the higher path and follow the directions given in Walk 1 from 'Follow the path across the fellside' to 'far blue mountains of Lakeland'.

Now return across the saddle to the Atkinson Pike cairn. Descend a shaly path north-westerly over Blue Screes which runs out on to the pleasant ridge, mainly grassy with the odd slaty outcropping, which curves north-easterly down on to the grassy saddle at the head of the Glenderamackin valley. En route it gives you an interesting and less publicised view of Sharp Edge. Cross the saddle and follow a faint path up the far slope. Shortly take a right fork, which soon sinks without trace into swampy ground. Continue just south of east to reach the cairn crowning the summit of Bannerdale Crags, 2230 feet.

Now head north-west to pick up a good path following the rim of the crags falling into Bannerdale. A path climbing out of Bannerdale is crossed and beyond it easy grass leads north to the cairn and wind shelter crowning Bowscale Fell, 2306 feet.

Descend just east of north to reach the lip of the combe cupping Bowscale Tarn. An interesting rake slants across the steep rough southern flank of the combe and is gained by a loose earthy slope. Once on it follow the slanting rake across the fellside to its end, then head directly down steep grass to the shore of the tarn. A path leads around the tarn to its outlet beck. Should you not fancy the rake, descend north along the rim of Tarn Crags until you are above the outlet beck. Descend steep grass to and across the beck to join the path on its far bank.

Follow this path in a slanting descent across the fellside, overlooking the River Caldew, to emerge on to the road near the hamlet of Bowscale. Turn right and follow the road back to Mungrisdale.

Walk 3

10 miles
6000 feet of ascent

# Five Blencathra Ridges

*This is one for the genuine dedicated 'nutcase' fellwalker. This alternate up and down traverse of Blease Fell, Gategill Fell, Hall's Fell, Doddick Fell and Scales Fell could be said to be a gimmick more than a walk. I feel, however, that a guidebook writer should be continually trying to offer his readers variety and a challenge. With a little imagination it's possible to do this even in a Lakeland whose bookshops are packed with guidebooks and whose fells are crowded with walkers. Anyway, if a geriatric like me can do it, anybody can!*

*Parking/Start: As for Walk 1.*

FOLLOW the directions for Walk 1 as far as the first gate. Beyond it turn left along a path to reach the rocky banks of Scaley Beck. Cross the beck and continue with the path alongside a wall to a fork. Take the left fork down to a gate, pass through it and continue to a gate leading on to the bank of Doddick Gill. Cross the gill and continue alongside the wall to reach the weir at the foot of Gategill. Cross the weir and climb up to a gate in a wall corner. Pass through this and follow a path across a field to a stile. Beyond this go down to a gate leading on to the bank of Blease Gill. Beyond rises the ridge of Blease Fell. Look for a green path climbing on to the lower end of this ridge. To reach it cross the beck and climb alongside a wall to a gate. Climb the steepening path beyond until the angle eases and the path forks. Take the right, fainter, path which ultimately expires on a grassy shoulder giving a fine view over the head of Blease Gill. Now climb left up steepening grass to emerge on to the crest of the ridge and a good path. Westward, Lonscale Fell attempts to look like a proper mountain against a backcloth of Skiddaw's grassy domes. Above the wooded isles of Derwentwater rise an array of elegantly indented fells.

Climb right to reach the summit of Blease Fell. Continue along the fell rim into a dip then up on to the 851 metre summit overlooking the Gategill Fell ridge. It's perfectly obvious from here that any sane person would continue north-east along the fell rim for the short walk and climb to reach Blencathra top. Only an idiot would descend over two thousand rough feet to the weir at the foot of Hall's Fell, then climb up its steep, crenellated crest to arrive at the same point. It's my belief, however, that true mountain addicts march to the beat of a different drum whose tattoo insists that they be oftimes daft or venturesome. So with a cry of 'Geronimo' launch yourself down the shaly groove just beyond the 851 metre summit.

Slabby, scree-littered rocks lead left on to a slender grassy ridge, which leads down on to the broader, rock-spined crest of Gategill Fell. When the ridge widens, ignore the path bearing right, and keep to the left edge. An intermittent path presently drops steeply down the fell corner to vanish amongst the outcrops, loose scree fans, and wiry ankle-grasping heather of Blea Crags. I found this the roughest section of the walk and was relieved to flop down on the grassy bank near the weir and give my jellied knees a rest.

I'd decided at the outset that the climb up Hall's Fell would be the 'make or break' point for me. I felt that if I had made it to Blencathra top then I'd 'cracked' it. I took it very slowly, counting steps between 'breathers', and having a good rest and more sustenance at the foot of Narrow Edge. I actually began to enjoy myself and, taking advantage of a beautiful October day and the second wind I'd acquired from somewhere, took the more enjoyable, but more demanding, line up and down the rocky crest.

Once on Blencathra's painfully gained summit cairn walk right, then shortly right again when the path forks down on to a steepish grass slope. Below this the path eases out and passes behind a line of rocky outcrops overlooking the depths of Doddick Gill. Turn right into the gap before the last outcrop and down into a shaly groove. This slants left along the base of rocks on to the crest of Doddick Fell. The descent of this ridge is straighforward, with only a couple of easy rock steps to clamber down. When the ridge eases out, look for a grassy path forking left through the bracken. Follow this easily down to reach the slabby crossing of Scaley Beck. Just above the rocks on the far bank turn left up a path through the bracken to begin your last big climb of the day.

Ignore any crossing paths and follow the path as it twists up towards the base of Goat Crags. Well below these it makes a long 'zig' to the right to emerge on to a grassy path 'zagging' leftwards. Climb left along this path, which leads, with one short 'zig' to the right, on to the grassy crest above Goat Crags, where it disappears. This is of no matter now, for it is simply a matter of climbing up this broad grassy south ridge of Scales Fell, keeping the depths of Scaley Beck to your left. The angle eases gradually and eventually a path is joined on the rim of Scales Fell.

Given a good day, there is a very rewarding view to your left as you climb. Ranked in burnished splendour towards the setting sun are the

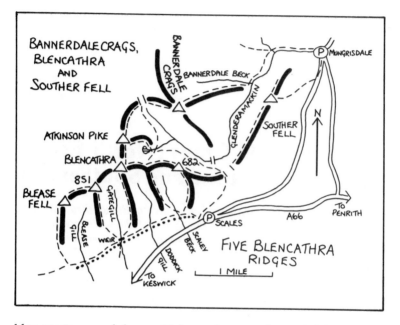

blue crests up and down which you have made a painful progress. Give them a cheery salute for you will never again drive along the A66 without glancing up at them with a grin, remembering this epic.

Continue leftwards along the undulating fell rim, over the 641 and 682 metre tops, before making the short steeper climb to the lip of the shaly groove where you launched yourself down on to Doddick Fell, thus completing the five ridges. From here a really fit walker would continue up to the summit of Blencathra before descending Sharp Edge in a truly worthy finale to a splendid walk. I didn't trust my wobbly old legs to get me safely across Sharp Edge, however. Having achieved what I'd set out to do, proving to my own satisfaction that there was life in the old dog yet, I headed down the grassy slope falling into Scales Tarn.

13

From Scales Tarn I followed the path down Scales Beck and along the north east flank of Scales Fell, above the Glenderamackin. Where it forks I climbed right before swinging right again above the deep hollow of Mousthwaite Comb. A steepish descent then led to the final slant right to the gate leading on to the A66. You wouldn't believe it, but on a beautiful October day, with dozens of fellwalkers beating their way to its door, the pub at Scales was shut!

**Walk 4**

**8 miles**
**2800 feet of ascent**

# Bannerdale Crags (North-East Ridge), Blencathra and Souther Fell

*An interesting off-the-beaten-track route to Blencathra that can easily be adapted to suit both the tastes of the walker who finds Sharp Edge too venturesome, and also the walker who can't wait to perch him or herself on a narrow rocky crest. Souther Fell gives a nice amiable finish to the day and unusual views back on to the peaks climbed. The Ordnance Survey, Landranger Series, Sheet 90, 1:50000, Penrith, Keswick and Ambleside map may be useful for this walk.*

*Parking/Start: As for Walk 2*

FOLLOW the directions for Walk 2 as far as the crossing of Bannerdale Beck. Now, after crossing this beck, leave the riverside path and climb right on to the crest of the grassy spur leading to the foot of the north east ridge of Bannerdale Crags. The final ridge is steep and rocky but all the difficulties can be avoided by keeping to the left of the crest. If you prefer a little excitement, however, climb the succession of slaty hummocks overlooking an impressive drop to the right. From the top of the ridge a short climb rightwards brings you to the summit cairn of Bannerdale Crags, 2230 feet.

Now descend just north of west over swampy, then steepening, grass to the saddle below the north east ridge of Blencathra. Climb this largely grassy ridge to a steep finish up a scree slope to emerge on to easier ground near the cairn crowning Atkinson Pike, 2772 feet, Blencathra's northern summit. (The more venturesome could cross the saddle then follow a path traversing left across the north east flank of Blencathra to reach Scales Beck. From here follow the description given in Walk 1, from 'Now climb the path alongside this beck' to 'Atkinson Pike, 2772 feet, Blencathra's northern summit'.) Either way, from Atkinson Pike continue with the description given in Walk 1, from 'A broad grassy ridge' to 'blue mountains of Lakeland'.

From Blencathra's top turn left, east, from the summit cairn, then shortly right when the path forks down on to a steepish grass slope. Below this the path eases out and passes behind a line of rocky outcrops overlooking the depths of Doddick Gill. Descend again beyond the last outcrop before climbing slightly then following the rim of Scales Fell, over its 682 and 641 metre tops. Beyond the latter head east down grassy slopes on to the saddle above Mousthwaite Comb.

Now climb north-easterly on to the broad grassy crest of Souther Fell, 1680 feet, and continue to the northern and highest summit. A ghostly army reputedly repeatedly marched across the crest of Souther fell in the late eighteenth century.

Ignore the path continuing beyond the summit and turn right down the steep grassy fellside for about three hundred feet to join a grassy unused path slanting left. Follow it pleasantly down to reach a tarmac road near a gate. Follow the road leftwards into Mungrisdale, conveniently passing the pub.

**Walk 5**

**13 miles**
**3000 feet of ascent**

# Back O' Skiddaw

*A splendid walk along the far northern and uncrowded rim of mountain Lakeland. On the tops, cairns are rare and paths intermittent, indistinct or non-existent: in bad weather, a good test of your skill in navigation. It has a reputation as a bog trot, but I've suffered much worse. Being on the edge of Lakeland, the views are different. All told, a rewarding 'bag' of seven 'two thousands', one of which may have been the stronghold of Iron Age 'freedom fighters'.*

*Parking/Start: On the grass verges either south or north of the hamlet of Mosedale. (GR357324).*

FROM Mosedale, walk along the public road, signposted 'Swineside', up the valley of the River Caldew to the road-end where the Carrock Fell mine road forks right. (Notice the hut on the skyline of Great Lingy Hill, above and to your right. From this hut there is a useful escape route from the tops should you need it). Continue up the valley along the riverside path, signposted 'Skiddaw House, etc.'. The bulk of Skiddaw blocks the valley ahead. At its foot a plantation shelters Skiddaw House, see Walk 8. As you go the valley of the Blackhazel Beck opens up across the Caldew, its source dominated by Atkinson Pike, Blencathra's northern summit.

About two miles from the road-end the path crosses a footbridge over Wiley Gill. Beyond rises the shapely outline of Great Calva, the steep direct line of an old boundary fence marking your way to its top. Beyond the bridge turn right, near an old sheepfold, past a cairn, and follow a faint path up the left bank of the gill. The grassy dome looming over the head of the gill is Knott. Shortly, you will reach the rusting fence hanging down a steep heathery bank. Haul yourself up alongside it on to easier ground and a crossing path. (I'm told if you go a little further up the gill an easier path leads to the same place). Now climb alongside the fence. It's a bit of a struggle and if it helps to get you up it you may, instead of counting steps, count the variety of ways the author might be slowly put to death. I don't mind, now you've bought the book! Be assured, there's nothing anywhere as hard on the rest of the walk.

Eventually you will wobble on to the surprisingly rocky summit of Great Calva, 2265 feet. Southwards, a distant Thirlmere gleams in the hollow of the great natural fault splitting Lakeland from Keswick to Windermere. Blencathra disappoints from this angle, but we'll forgive her because she enthrals and delights from elsewhere. Skiddaw looms large and lumpy. North-easterly, only Knott, High Pike and Carrock Fell of the six remaining 'two thousanders' display themselves in a skyline that looks deceptively flat.

Now head north-westerly alongside a fence. When it veers more westerly leave it and head north. You should soon pick up a boggy path leading down on to the saddle below Knott. A faint path now climbs north-easterly up steepish grass to the right of a gill – Burn Tod. When over the first crest turn left, across the head of Burn Tod. Follow a north-north-easterly heading across the tiresome tussocky west flank of Knott, above the slopes steepening into the bowl cupping the minor but piquantly named peaks of Great and Little Cockup.

This should bring you into a dip below Great Sca Fell, 2131 feet, a grassy, scruffy peasant of a fell masquerading under a proud and noble name. From its minisucle summit cairn return into the dip and climb south-easterly up a broad grassy ridge to reach the cairn crowning the grassy dome of Knott, at 2329 feet the high point of the walk. A feature of the view from here is the dark prow of the Isle of Man thrusting around the northern end of Skiddaw's great whaleback.

Now walk north east to the fell rim falling into the swampy reaches of Miller Moss. Rising to the north of the swamps, and overlooking the long defile of Roughton Gill, is the lowly, table-like summit mound of Miller Moss. East of this rises the infinitesimally higher dome of Great Lingy Hill, with the hut marking the escape route mentioned earlier perched on its southern skyline.

Descend the steep grass and follow the watershed between the more obvious swamps oozing right, down into Grainsgill beck, and the becks spilling north off Knott into Roughton Gill. At the lowest point the peaty waters of a beck are crossed before a short heathery climb leads to the small cairn crowning Miller Moss, 2000 feet.

Look east from here to pick out a patch of bouldery scree just below the skyline of Great Lingy Hill's heathery dome. The miniscule summit cairn stands to the left of this. To reach it head into a dip then up through a mat of heather. From Great Lingy Hill, 2000 feet, descend east to join a path. A turn right here would lead you past the hut previously mentioned and subsequently down to the road-end. Given good conditions, however, it would be a pity to use this 'escape' route with so much of the walk accomplished. So turn left and follow the path, marked 'Cumbria Way' on the map, over a rise then down rightwards across the south flank of High Pike. Ignore faint paths to right and left until just above and to the left of the eroded head of Carrock Beck, where paths fork left and right. Climb the left fork to reach the trig-point and slate memorial seat crowning High Pike, 2157 feet.

Return the same way, cross the Cumbria Way, and follow the 'right fork' passing above and to the right of the eroded bank of Carrock Beck. This path leads on to the crest of the broad switchback ridge running easterly and culminating in the shapely, stony summit of Carrock Fell, 2174 feet. As you go, across the depths of the Caldew, shadows pool in the high combe of Bowscale Tarn. Far away to the south-west Gable's blue cone dominates the gap between the Skiddaw and Blencathra whalebacks.

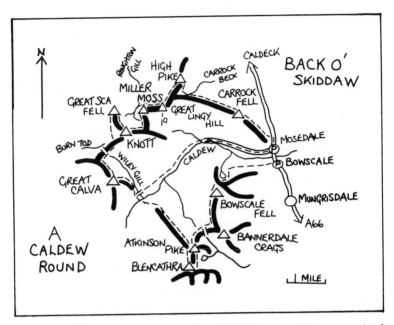

What appears to be a decrepit sheepfold built around the summit of Carrock Fell is reputedly an Iron Age fort. It has been suggested it was a centre of British resistance to the Roman invaders and that the gaps in its walls were breaches made when the legions finally stormed in. More likely they're due to clumsy fellwalkers. Still, it's warming to think of our woad-spattered forefathers squatting here plying their iron toothpicks – dinosaur steak must have been pretty stringy – whilst planning raids! Perhaps the vanished Ninth Legion was ambushed and annihilated somewhere under Carrock Fell by a horde of hairy mead louts . . .

Descend through the fort's 'east gate' and follow a narrow path twisting south-easterly down through thick heather to reach the rim of a steep grassy gully. Descend the gully to where a path slants left across the fellside on to easy grass leading on to the road. From the gully rim downwards is a bit 'knee-jellying' and I'm told that if you move right, across the head of the gully, a somewhat less arduous descent takes you down to the roadside. Turn right and follow the road back to Mosedale.

# A Caldew Round

*It must be obvious to the map reader that a complete Caldew Horseshoe, starting and finishing at Bowscale or Mosedale, and taking in the Blencathra, Skiddaw and Back O'Skiddaw groups, would make a superb mountain marathon. So far this walk has eluded me. Well, to be honest, I think it's been more a matter of me eluding it. I've twice set out with good intentions but on both occasions opted out of the Skiddaw group, either through laziness or lack of fitness. The end result of both attempts was the walk described below, which is, nevertheless, a fine walk in its own right.*

*Parking/Start: As for Walk 5*

WALK south up the road to Bowscale. Where the road passes between buildings and turns left you turn right through a gate and follow the path which subsequently climbs across the fellside above the Caldew Valley to reach the shore of Bowscale Tarn near its exit beck. Walk left around the tarn. The far bank rises in a steep slope of rock, grass and scree. Slanting from left to right across this slope is an obvious rake. Climb up steep grass to reach the lower end of the rake and climb it to a shaly finish up on to the grassy rim of the fell. If for any reason you don't fancy this rake turn right across the exit beck and reach the fell rim by a steep grassy climb to the right of the crags. Either way, now head south up grassy slopes to reach the summit cairn of Bowscale Fell, 2306 feet.

Descend southerly to meet a crossing path emerging over the fell rim overlooking Bannerdale. Cross this and follow a path along the curving rim of Bannerdale. When it ends continue along the rim to shortly reach the summit cairn of Bannerdale Crags, 2230 feet. Now head just north of west down to the grassy saddle at the foot of the north east ridge of Blencathra. Climb this ridge, which ends in a shaly finish to reach the summit cairn of Atkinson Pike, 2772 feet, Blencathra's northern top. Head south, across the 'saddle' and past the quartz cross, to reach the summit cairn of Blencathra, 2847 feet. A more detailed description of this section will be found in Walk 1, from 'Atkinson Pike, 2772 feet, Blencathra's northern summit'.

Walk back across the saddle to Atkinson Pike. Now descend north-west across the broad trackless grassland of Mungrisdale Common, followed by a steeper finish down Long Brow, to cross the Caldew just above its junction with Wiley Gill. Walk up the left bank of Wiley Gill to cross the Cumbria Way footpath near an old sheepfold. Continue up the gill to where an old rusting fence hangs down the steep heathery bank on your left. Now follow the directions given in Walk 5, from 'Haul yourself up alongside it' to its end in Mosedale.

# SKIDDAW

**Walk 7**

**7 miles**
**3000 feet of ascent**

## Skiddaw via Longside Edge

*Almost invariably the 'tourist' routes to the tops of the major
Lakeland fells are the most uninteresting. The Jenkin Path up
Skiddaw is no exception to this rule, being a long boring trudge.
Offered below is a more varied and entertaining way to Skiddaw's
hoary and boot-battered dome.*

*Parking/Start: In the Forestry Association Dodd Wood/Mirehouse
Sawmill car park on the A591 Keswick/Carlisle road, just over four
miles north west of Keswick. (GR235282).*

RETURN to the A591 and turn right. Follow its right-hand verge for
just under a mile to reach a narrow fenced path climbing steeply up
between the northern edge of Dodd Wood and the wooded grounds of
the Ravenstone Hotel.

Climb this path, bearing left, to reach a gate/stile leading on to the
open fellside. Continue up the obvious path bearing leftwards along
the edge of a wood. Ignore a faint path forking right and continue on to
where a cairn marks a path fork. Take the right-hand path which twists
steeply upwards to reach the crest of a ridge. Beyond the crest lies the
bleak upland valley of Southerndale, dominated by the massive scree-
capped dome of Skiddaw.

Turn right and follow the ridge, climbing towards the graceful and
beckoning cone of Ullock Pike, 2230 feet. From the summit of Ullock
Pike the entire gleaming, yacht-speckled length of Bassenthwaite
Lake is spread below. North-westerly, the green Cumbrian flatlands
and the grey Solway Firth stretch away to meet Scotland, whilst
southwards a magnificent jumble of peaks are jammed between south-
easterly Catstycam and south-westerly Whiteside.

Beyond Ullock Pike continue pleasantly along the grassy and slaty
crest of Longside Edge, 2405 feet. Compared to the Super League
ridges of Sharp, Striding and Hall's Fell this is a Scunthorpe United
kind of an 'edge'. Plain fare, but enjoyable for all that. It ends in a dip

beyond which rises the heathery dome of Carlside. The path now edges leftwards along the rim of Southerndale, bypassing the summit of Carlside, to reach a grassy saddle, crowned by tiny Carlside Tarn, below the south top of Skiddaw. Climb left from the saddle up a path slanting across the steep shaly west flank of Skiddaw, overlooking Southerndale. The path steepens, then bears right into a hollow on the broad summit ridge behind the south top. Turn left and climb over the central, 928 metre, top to reach the cairn and trig-point crowning the northern and highest summit of Skiddaw, 3054 feet.

The view from Skiddaw is remarkable more for its extent than its detail. It's an ideal location for the enthusiastic fell-spotter to attempt to orientate him or herself to all the splendid humpety and bumpety spread around and below. I'll presume to give you a couple of clues. Helvellyn is approximately south-south-east and Gable is approximately south-south-west. Skiddaw has long been a popular climb. A Bishop of Carlisle climbed it in 1684 and five years later a small observatory was set up on the summit. On the evening of August 21st, 1815, the Southeys and the Wordsworths and an entourage of friends and helpers lit a bonfire and had a 'knees-up' on the summit to celebrate the victory at Waterloo.

Now return down to the saddle of Carlside Tarn. From here climb south-westerly and easily over slaty rocks to reach the summit cairn of Carlside, 2420 feet. Beyond this follow a path bearing leftwards, south, which descends the fell's south ridge just below and to the left of its crest. Leftwards the ground falls steeply away into a gill, with the shapely outlier of Carsleddam rising across its depths. Beyond and below lie the rooftops of Keswick, gleaming island-pocked Derwentwater, and the dark Jaws of Borrowdale. The path heads down towards the obvious natural feature of White Stones. Just before reaching this turn right along a fainter path flanking across the heathery fellside. Below looms wooded Dodd. Shortly a path forks leftwards and down. Descend this to reach a stile in a fence leading on to the forest road crowning Long Doors, the narrow saddle dividing Carlside and Dodd.

Turn right to shortly pass a waymarked path climbing left up the flank of Dodd. It's been my practice to finish off this walk with an ascent of Dodd. On my last visit, tree-felling barred access to Dodd up this flank and was obviously destroying the dark, needle-carpeted aisles that were a unique contrast to the bare flanks of Skiddaw. How the situation stands at this moment of writing I cannot say. The path, its character destroyed, may have been re-opened or diversions posted. Should you choose to add Dodd I must, unfortunately, leave you to your own devices. Otherwise, continue down the forest road which subsequently forks to take either bank of Skill Beck. Follow the right fork which shortly divides again with a built up forest road branching right. Keep to the lower and left fork, above the beck, and follow it down to reach a wooden footbridge leading across the beck and into the car park.

**Walk 8**                                               **10 miles**
**2500 feet of ascent**
**(Add 3 miles and 600 feet**
**of ascent if you start and**
**finish in Keswick)**

# Skiddaw via Skiddaw House

*This walk is an interesting variation on the 'tourist' route up and down the Jenkin Path. Slightly longer perhaps, but not appreciably harder, it offers contrasting aspects of Skiddaw. The ascent follows a delightful path into a vast bowl of bare fells where the weathered walls of Skiddaw House are tucked into the shelter of a dark copse. Infrequently visited Lonscale Fell is climbed and the 'tourist' route joined for the final climb to Skiddaw, and the descent.*

*Parking/Start: In the car park where the minor road ends behind Latrigg. (GR281254). From the roundabout on the A66 just north-west of Keswick take the A591 Carlisle/Bothel road. Almost immediately turn right up the minor road signposted 'Ormathwaite/ Underscar'. Follow this road to a sharp right-hand bend below the Gale Hotel. Turn right here and follow the steep rough road up to the car park.*

*Pedestrians from Keswick follow the A591 Carlisle/Bothel out of the town to where a minor road, signposted 'Railway Station. Latrigg/ Skiddaw', forks right. Follow this to see on your left a signpost 'Public Bridleway/Skiddaw'. This path leads to a footbridge over the A66 and subsequently on up the western flank of Latrigg to the car park described above.*

LEAVE the car park by the gate signposted 'Skiddaw/Bassenthwaite /Mosedale'. A path between fences leads to a gate/stile beyond which the path forks. Take the right hand, grassier, path which goes around a corner then down to and across Whit Beck. Beyond the beck it climbs gradually across the broad grassy south flank of Lonscale Fell. To your right, Clough Head leads the procession of peaks marching south towards Helvellyn. Glance over your right shoulder and see Derwentwater edging into view behind Latrigg. Ahead rises Blease Fell, Blencathra's western outlier.

The path eventually swings north on to slaty ledges beneath Lonscale Crags and overlooking the deep narrow valley of the Glenderaterra Beck. Ahead rise Great Calva and Knott. Look back down the great natural fault sheltering the A591 for a glimpse of Thirlmere. Across the valley Blencathra's summit comes into view at the head of the grassy trough of Roughton Gill, a bare, bleak, massive Blencathra that contrasts vividly with the elegantly sculpted, excitingly ridged mountain described earlier in this book. The ridge rising leftwards ahead, crowned by a fence, is Burnt Horse, your prospective route to Lonscale Fell. A stony section leads down to and across a beck, beyond which the path from Threlkeld is joined. Turn left and climb alongside a wall, then across more open boggy ground, to reach a gate in a wall at the foot of Burnt Horse.

Skiddaw House, set in its dark woody wind shelter, now comes into view. Beyond the gate boggy ground leads to a bridge over Salehow Beck. Cross it and climb leftwards to a gap in the wall enclosing the copse. Continue up, passing between old iron gateposts, to reach Skiddaw House. This formerly derelict building has recently been opened up as a Youth Hostel, and become the centre of controversy. Temporarily closed on our last visit, we took advantage of the notice inviting us to use the open bothy to have lunch. On a bleak December day it was easy to visualise the lives of past dwellers here as hard and lonely. Oftimes it must have been, but oftimes too, for those with open eyes, ears and hearts, it must have been infinitely rewarding.

Return through the gateposts and the gap in the wall and turn right alongside the wall until it encroaches close to the bank of Salehow Beck. Now cross the beck and climb up alongside an old fence to join the fence and wall crowning Burnt Horse. Turn right and climb this ridge which culminates in a grassy dip. Cross this and follow the fence up the steep far slope. The angle eventually eases and a fence corner is reached. Climb over the corner and follow a faint path left to reach the cairn crowning the grassy dome of Lonscale Fell, 2344 feet. Walk a little further north-easterly to a cairn perched on the rim of Lonscale Crags for a 'birds-eye' view of your approach route.

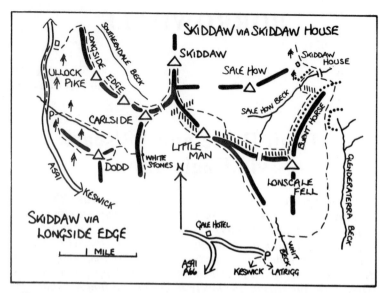

Return to the fence corner and re-cross it. Now follow a path alongside the westerly heading fence on to the boggy saddle of Flag Pots. A gate on your left here offers an escape route back to the car park should you feel the need. Follow the fence north-westerly up on to Jenkin Hill, where it veers westerly again to join the 'tourist' path at a stile. Now turn right and follow this eroded highway around the flanks of Little Man and up to a gate/stile in a fence below the south summit of Skiddaw. Climb this top and head north over the intervening 928 metre top to reach the trig point and cairn crowning Skiddaw, 3054 feet. (See Walk 7 for a brief historical and scenic description.)

Return to the fence below the south summit. If you are still feeling energetic ignore the 'tourist' route and turn right alongside the fence to shortly follow it left down on to a saddle below Little Man. Climb alongside the fence then veer right to reach the cairn crowning Little Man, 2837 feet. The view, especially of Derwentwater, Borrowdale, and their encircling fells, is superior to that on Skiddaw, and worth the extra effort entailed. Descend left to reach the fence and follow it down to rejoin the 'tourist' path where it passes through the fence. Turn right and follow the eroded path down to the car park.

If you are still feeling energetic, leave the car park by the path leading down to Keswick and turn immediately left along a path climbing on to the grassy dome of Latrigg for an even better view of Keswick, Derwentwater and Borrowdale.

# BORROWDALE

**Walk 9**

**9 miles**
**3000 feet of ascent**

# High Raise and Ullscarf via Eagle Crag

*The Stonethwaite valley is dominated by Eagle Crag. It's rugged cone draws the eye and offers an irresistible challenge to climber and walker alike. Its ascent offers an enjoyable prelude to the ascent of two somewhat swampy 'puddens' that are nevertheless fine viewpoints, having other more secretive charms. I've frequently spotted deer on Ullscarf and a couple of fine foxes lolloping over its bogs. Given their due season, the lovely Bogbean and Bog Asphodel, the insectivorous Sundew and Butterwort, and similar wetland plants could be spotted. Dock Tarn, a lovely but unacclaimed upland tarn, delightfully rounds off the day.*

*Parking/Start: From Keswick follow the Borrowdale road, B5289, for about 6½ miles to reach the Stonewaite turn-off. Follow this to pass a terrace of white houses and a school. Park in lay-bys just beyond the school or just ahead in Stonethwaite by the telephone kiosk. (GR261139).*

WHEN the medieval Cistercians of Fountains and Furness Abbeys had Borrowdale nicely parcelled out between them Stonethwaite was a thriving dairy farm, or 'vaccary'. A dispute arose about ownership and the matter was put before the king. Edward 1, as well as being the 'Hammer of the Scots', was not renowned for his charity towards his own countrymen, not even monks. He promptly confiscated Stonethwaite then sold it back to the highest clerical bidder. Turn left at the telephone kiosk and walk between buildings to cross the Stonethwaite Bridge. On the far bank turn right, following the signpost 'Grasmere via Greenup Edge'. Pass a metal 'Dock Tarn' sign, your return route, and continue up the valley. Pass above the Galleny Force waterfall and, higher, the confluence of Langstrath Beck and Greenup Gill. Just above this meeting of waters go through a gate on your right and down to and across a footbridge spanning Greenup Gill. Climb up the far bank shortly to turn left across a stile in a fence.

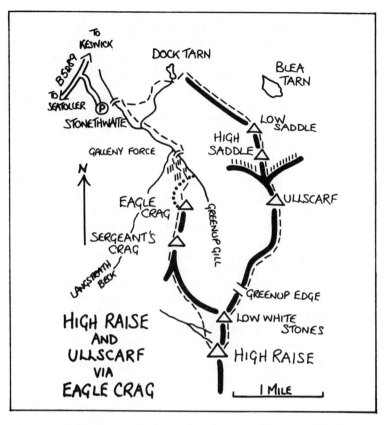

Continue to a gate. Follow the path beyond to a scramble through a gap in a wall. Now turn right up the steep brackeny fellside overlooked by the towering rocks of Eagle Crag. Grind upwards and the path becomes more obvious and reaches the base of the rocks near a wall. Cross a stile in a length of fence blocking the gap between the wall and the crag. The path soon climbs left up a rocky gully. At its head follow a path to the right which then twists upwards around rocky outcrops to eventually emerge on to the cairn-crowned rock slab that's the summit of Eagle Crag, 1600 feet.

Eagle and Sergeant Crags rest on a broad spur dividing the deep crag-lined valley of Langstrath, and its sinuously gleaming beck, from a bleak swampy combe feeding the Greenup Gill. From Eagle Crag head along the spur, south then south-westerly, passing a wall corner, following the wall a little way, then veering right up on to the rocky summit of Sergeant Crag, 1873 feet.

Beyond Sergeant Crag a faint path drops south then soon forks. Take the fainter path forking left climbing south-easterly towards the summit of High Raise, which is the right hand and apparently lowest of the summits crowning the skyline above. It's best hereabouts to rely on your map and the lie of the ground rather than hunt for paths, which have a tendency to disappear or run across your heading. It's a steady slanting plod which passes well to the right of Long Crag's angular rocks, close under the rocks supporting the subsidiary summit of Low White Stones, and across the head of a couple of nameless becks before emerging close to the trig-point and wind shelter crowning High Raise, 2500 feet.

High Raise, or High White Stones as it was more commonly called when I was a mountain mad lad, is a dreary swampy plateau which being centrally placed is a fine viewpoint. From High Raise head north-east then north to cross the rocky top of Low White Stones. Then head north-easterly down on to the saddle of Greenup Edge. Old iron fence stanchions intermittently mark the way. In thick mist rely more on your compass, using the stanchions as a back-up. Greenup Edge is an ancient Lakeland highway. The Cistercians had licence to pack wool clips, dairy produce and salt from their Borrowdale holdings over to the mother houses. The late Graham Sutton, an entertaining but unfortunately largely forgotten Lakeland writer, described Greenup Edge as 'the soggiest sponge in Lakeland'.

Cross the saddle and crowning path to climb in a north-north-east, north-east and northerly dog-leg, alongside the old stanchions, to reach the cairn crowning Ullscarf, 2370 feet. Leave the cairn and follow the path and stanchions west of north to reach the corner of a recently erected wood and wire fence. Turn left and follow the fence down to where it veers left again. Now cross a stile in the fence and follow a faint path just west of north down a broad grassy ridge into a dip below the rocky summit of High Saddle. Down to your right now Blea Tarn points its gleaming assegai blade towards the distant Solway.

Climb over High Saddle and continue down in the same line to cross over the crest of Low Saddle. The path swings left of this top but it's worth the short climb for the unusual view of Watendlath Tarn, a slice of Derwentwater, Bassenthwaite Lake and the far Solway in line ahead. Away to your left Eagle Crag and Sergeant Crag tower above shadowy Langstrath. Below, to the north-west, Dock Tarn, your next target, peeps behind a range of dark hillocks. Pick a gap in these hillocks and head for it, for the faint path soon disappears into a swampy 'Empty Quarter'. On a recent crossing here a golden plover burst from virtually under my boots, leaving a downy chick crouched under a tussock, motionless save for its frantic but barely perceptible heartbeats.

Once across and through the gap a short descent to and around Dock Tarn leads on to a path along its far shore. A lovely armada of water lilies graced its rock-girt waters on my last visit. Turn left and follow the path down to the rim of the Stonethwaite valley. Across its depths the rocky tors of Bessyboot, Rosthwaite Cam, Doves Nest Top and Combe Head rise in column of march to the craggy crest of Glaramara. Continue down through woodland on a steep reconstructed path, which leaves ageing knees a bit hot and blancmangy, to emerge on to your outward route.

**Walk 10**                                                    **11 miles**
**3200 feet of ascent**

# Bessyboot, Glaramara and Allen Crags

*Glaramara does not appear in the top fifty highest Lakeland fells, nor is it one of the most visually exciting, 'knobbly' being perhaps the most descriptive word for it. Yet it is one of my favourite fells, offering variety and entertainment to scrambler, climber and fellwalker alike. Climb every rocky knobble on the ridge walk described below, enjoying every sublime view, and return down the long lovely trough of Langstrath having tasted a little of what this fine fell can offer.*

*Parking/Start: As for Walk 9*

WALK through Stonethwaite, passing the Langstrath Hotel, and follow a rough track climbing slightly right. Just beyond a culvert, and before the entrance to the campsite, turn right through a metal gate in the fence to your right. Beyond it climb the path twisting steeply up through the trees, alongside Big Stanger Gill. A stile in a wall at the entrance of a ravine is reached and crossed. Follow the path across the rough and stony fellside below Alisongrass Crag to reach and round the end of a wall. Continue along the gill bank to a cairn near the end of a wall. Go through a gap in the wall, opposite the cairn, and follow a path up the left bank of the gill which has now turned sharply right (west).

At a cairn below a small cascade cross the gill and scramble up the far bank to a cairn. Turn left now and follow a faint path along the right bank into a grassy combe surrounded by rocky hummocks. Follow the path and the diminishing beck in a climb towards the righthand end of a rocky ridge ahead. Go around the end of this ridge to a cairn on a boulder with a path on its right. Go to the left of this cairn to find a pool set at the foot of a slabby ridge. Turn left beyond the pool and follow the base of the rocks on your left up into a gap between hillocks. In the gap climb right to reach the summit of Bessyboot, 1807 feet.

The view, dramatically sudden, is superb. Highlights are the stark profile and gutted flank of Honister Crag, and away to the south the far blue cone of Pike O'Stickle. Below lies the austere but delightfully named Tarn at Leaves, with the pinnacled crest of Rosthwaite Cam rising beyond. (The objective of the exercise now, particularly for the peak bagger, is to climb every rocky knobble over two thousand feet high from Rosthwaite Cam to Allen Crags. The number vary depending upon which list you tick. The ridge from Bessyboot to Glaramara could require careful navigation in bad conditions, for the path is faint and intermittent and the ground complicated.)

Descend into the grassy hollow beyond Bessyboot and follow a path climbing above and to the right of Tarn at Leaves. Leave this soon and climb a fainter path slanting right to reach the challenging summit pinnacle of Rosthwaite Cam, 2007 feet. Walk left along its base then scramble right, then right again over jammed blocks, to reach the cairn and a fine view down the wooded strath of Borrowdale to glinty Derwentwater. Across the depths of Combe Ghyll, Raven Crag thrusts from the flank of Thornthwaite Fell. Many climbers are first lured to its vegetated buttresses and dank gullies by Bentley Beetham's entertaining creation 'Corvus'.

Now head south-easterly to the next obvious 'knobble' on the ridge, which is unnamed on the map but listed as Doves Nest Top, 2066 feet. (From here it can be seen that Glaramara's summit is guarded by the rocky barrier of Comb Head, overlooking the bowl of Combe Gill and split by the gap of Comb Door. Look for an obvious grassy break in the crest of the skyline rocks away to the left of Comb Door. This is your next objective.)

Drop left from Dove Nest Top's rocky summit perch then turn right along a faint path which soon passes through a gap in an old wall. Beyond the wall the path goes to the left of a small tarn then twists around grassy hollows and rocky hummocks. At a fork bear left and climb around the base of crags and aprons of bouldery scree until the grassy break previously described comes into view ahead. Climb into

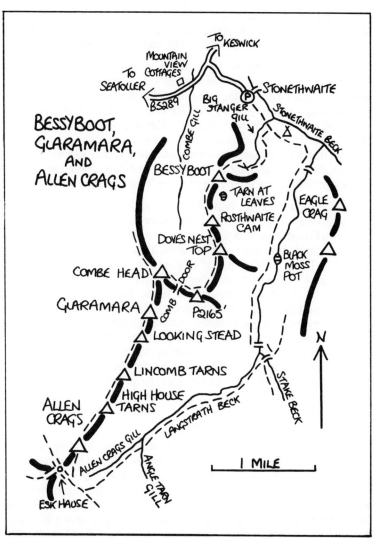

this break and from its crest climb right along a rocky ridge whose 660 metre/2165 feet high point is listed as a separate peak. This ridge sinks into the swampy tarnlet-crowned saddle of Comb Door. Slosh across this and climb up the grass and bouldery breach in the crags beyond. Follow a faint path climbing right out of the breach and on to a rocky ridge which leads to the cairn crowning Comb Head, 2394 feet. Northwards, the ground falls steeply into the drumlin-dimpled depths of Combe Gill. Doves Nest Caves are hidden amongst pallid rocks, marked by a tall rock pinnicle, on the combe's eastern flank. They were formed aeons ago when the crag slid partially down the fellside, creating a warren of fissures and subterranean passages.

Now descend south-westerly, across swampy ground, to join the well worn 'tourist' path from Mountain View Cottages, and follow this leftwards to the base of the summit rocks. A steepish but enjoyable scramble soon leads you to the Glaramara cairn, 2560 feet. From Glaramara 'every prospect pleases'. Borrowdale stretches verdantly away towards the plump grassy pleats of Skiddaw. With luck, the Isle of Man might be glimpsed moored on the port side of Gable. An easy escape route at this point in the walk is to return down the 'tourist' route over Thornthwaite Fell and down to Mountain View Cottages.

From Glaramara the summit ridge undulates two south-westerly miles towards Allen Crags and the encircling giants of Bowfell, Esk Pike and Great End. The path, a good one, has a tendency to be lazy, however, and takes the easy way around Looking Stead, 2542 feet, Lincomb Tarns, 2360 feet, and High House Tarns, 2244 feet, so the peak bagger who wishes to collect these tops must not be lulled into inaction by its amiable twists and turns. Remain vigilant for the sneaked-past summit. One of the many delights of this high level ridge are the tiny but delectable tarns set amidst the rocky tors. The word 'tarn' has Norse roots in 'tjorn', meaning 'tear'. Lakeland's tarns seen as 'tears of the mountains' is a pleasing whimsy. Allen Crags, 2570 feet, which brings the ridge to a stony full stop, tends to be overshadowed by its higher and craggier neighbours. I once climbed it in a 'white-out' and suddenly popped out of the murk to find myself above a sea of cloud from which the ice-masked giants of Lakeland thrust glinting cones and domes.

Drop south-west from Allen Crags to join the eroded path that climbs from Angle Tarn to Esk Hause just below and to the left of the wind shelter familiar to a host of fellwalkers. Turn left down this path into a dip. Turn left here and descend the right bank of the infant beck spilling into Allen Crags Gill. When the ground steepens a cairn will be spotted below. From it, cairns mark a thin path down the steep rough fellside to the right of the rocky ravine of Allen Crags Gill.

Eventually, to the relief of your knees, the path levels out into the Langstrath drumlins. Follow a faint path along the right bank of Langstrath Beck to join a better path on the far bank of the converging Angle Tarn Gill. Follow this alongside the Langstrath Beck to reach the footbridge over Stake Beck. Cross this and bear left down to a footbridge over the Langstrath Beck above the fine pool of Tray Dub. Ahead, a buttress of pallid rock rises steeply to a pinnacled crest. This is Cam Crag Ridge, which gives scramblers an entertaining option en route to Glaramara.

Follow the path down the valley, passing below Cam Crag Ridge, to reach a stile to the left of a sheepfold. Momentarily ignore this stile and walk right, past the fold, to find yourself on the rocky rim of Black Moss Pot, perhaps the most splendid natural bathing pool in Lakeland. I admit I've only swum in it once. Lacking the nerve to dive into its chilly green depths, I did a wimpish breaststroke up the shallow exit gorge. I hurriedly floundered out again when I was depth-charged by a pack of Wolf Cubs who hurled themselves off the sheer rim of the east bank with screams of 'Geronimo' and 'Banzai'.

Return to and cross the stile for the last couple of miles to Stonethwaite. The going is easy, if a bit stony under fell-flayed feet, but given a lovely summer evening the surroundings are superb. Bird song, the querulous calls of lambs and sheep, and the music of cascading water, Lakeland's signature tune, float up the sun-washed rock tiers of Heron and Sergeant Crags, and a pint of refreshing tea or beer awaits you in Stonethwaite.

**Walk 11**

**16 miles**
**1200 feet of ascent**

# A Borrowdale Walkabout

*I thought of slipping this valley walk in under the pretence that it was offered as a bad weather walk. Sixteen miles, however, is a bit much in bad weather, even over good low level paths. In the end I've included it simply because it's a splendid walk through varied terrain and scenery. Its length makes it as tough as some of the mountain walks described, thus ensuring that you won't feel guilty about not spending your day on the tops. One to do when autumn drapes its coat of many colours over the Borrowdale fells and woods.*

*Parking/Start: The National Trust car park in Seatoller. (GR245137).*

CLIMB out of the rear of the car park and turn right. Shortly the path forks. Follow the right fork down, behind 'Glaramara', to a gate. Beyond this, pass above Folly Bridge. Gates lead to a narrow fenced passage leading around an outcrop and on to some slabby rocks and a delightful scramble alongside the tumbling waters of the Derwent. Pass Longthwaite Youth Hostel and go down its drive on to a tree-lined riverside path signposted 'Permissive footpath towards Keswick'. I'm an inexpert birdwatcher but along this path I've spotted dippers, redstarts, goldfinches, wagtails, and a great spotted woodpecker.

Pass stepping stones bridging the Derwent. Here we were once treated to a charming vignette of Lakeland life. A tall, bearded shepherd, crook in one hand and blond toddler son clasped in the curve of his other arm, drove a flock of vociferous sheep across the river. It was an incredibly noisy scene. Plaintively protesting lambs plopped successively off the stepping stones like woolly depth charges. The little boy shrieked with laughter as his father bellowed at his dogs who tore back and forth across the river, like a pair of berserk destroyers trying to chivvy their convoy into some kind of formation.

Cross a footbridge over Tongue Gill and emerge from the trees near New Bridge. Walk past New Bridge to pass through the right hand of a pair of gates and continue along the river bank. At a fork beyond a clapper bridge (a stone slab straddling a beck) bear right along the river bank to a stile. You are now entering the Jaws of Borrowdale, where the pellucid Derwent and the B5289 are squeezed between the vegetated flanks of Castle Crag and King's How. Keep along the river bank to shortly enjoy some pleasant scrambling over two rocky outcrops thrusting into the river. The first is surmounted by climbing left to a wall end, then up polished slabs with the aid of a tree. The second can be climbed leftwards, but a line of narrow holds curving right, above the swirling water, give an exciting traverse, which is easier than it looks. Beyond, delightful riverside walking leads to a gate. (If flooding bars your way return across the stile and move left to a parallel path through the woods).

Beyond the gate a path forks left, signposted 'Bridleway – Seatoller/ Honister'. Ignore it and continue ahead into a campsite to join a rough track on the left of a wall. Pass through a gap, beyond which, on your left, a sign reads 'No Camping etc.'. Join a tarmac lane and turn right along it to subsequently enter Grange-in-Borrowdale. A 'grange' was a farm or granary held by a monastery. Turn left up the road, for just under a mile, to a gate on your right signposted 'Public footpath to Lodore'. Go through this gate, a further gate, and an opening in a fence, to a path fork.

Follow the right fork over a catwalk bridging a bog and follow the path beyond to reach the shore of Derwentwater. Turn right on to more catwalks leading to a footbridge over the Derwent, and beyond

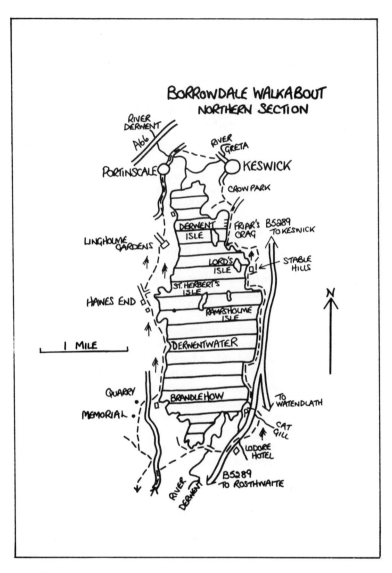

BORROWDALE WALKABOUT
NORTHERN SECTION

RIVER DERWENT
A66
RIVER GRETA
PORTINSCALE
KESWICK
CROW PARK
DERWENT ISLE
FRIAR'S CRAG
B5289 TO KESWICK
LINGHOLME GARDENS
LORD'S ISLE
STABLE HILLS
ST. HERBERT'S ISLE
HAWES END
RAMPSHOLME ISLE
DERWENTWATER
N
1 MILE
QUARRY
BRANDLEHOW
TO WATENDLATH
MEMORIAL
CAT GILL
LODORE HOTEL
B5289 TO ROSTHWAITE
RIVER DERWENT

to a stile leading on to the B5289. Turn left. A short distance beyond the Lodore Hotel go through a gap in the wall on your right and turn left along a path through the woods, parallel to the road. After crossing a footbridge over Cat Gill turn left alongside the beck to subsequently cross the B5289 and enter the lakeside National Trust 'Kettlewell' car park.

Turn right in the car park and walk along the lakeshore. The path becomes grassier as it rounds the next point into Barrow Bay, overlooked by tree-plumed Walla Crag and starker, steeper Falcon Crag. Pass behind a landing stage then along a narrow strip of lakeshore clinging to the B5289 before rounding a wooded promontory and entering Calf Close Bay. The walk around this bay leads on to a further wooded cape pointing at tiny Rampsholme Island, reputedly named after the 'ramp', or wild garlic, which grew (or grows?) there.

When Stable Hills House is reached the path turns away from the lake to a gate leading on to a rough track. Turn left. When the track curves right move left down the bank and through a gate on the edge of The Ings, a National Trust wood. Follow the path through and around the wood to emerge on the shore of Strandshag Bay. The mouth of this bay is guarded by Lord's Island, once a residence of the ill-fated Jacobite Earls of Derwentwater. When the wooded promontory of Friar's Crag is reached follow a path forking left on to its point. Ruskin, whose memorial crowns Friar's Crag, maintained the view from it was the fifth finest in Europe. Fifth or fifty-fifth, there is undoubtedly magic in the limpid water, the dark moored islands, and the subtly carved and coloured fells.

Anchored almost alongside is large, timbered Derwent Isle. In the sixteenth century emigrant German miners were brought over to unearth the riches of Newlands, where lead and copper veins thirteen and nine feet thick were reported 'the best in England'. These skilled, travelled and highly paid foreigners were an attraction for local girls, causing some disenchantment amongst Tudor Cumbrian males. There were ugly scenes and at least one murder, and for a while the Germans were lodged on Derwent Isle for their own safety. Eventually they became accepted and intermarried. Beck, Moses, Calvert, Raisley and Caryus are just a handful of the anglicised German names surviving in Cumbria.

Return along the point on to the road passing the boat landing stages. Climb the rise beyond and look for a gate on your left in the railings of Crow Park. Go through this and follow the path across the grassy slope. Do not go along the path to Isthmus Bay but keep bearing right, around the park, to a gate leading on to a road close to the town rubbish dump. Turn right and follow the road past caravan sites, the rugby club and the bus station to join the Keswick main street. Turn left. After crossing a bridge over the River Greta turn left at a footpath sign 'Portinscale.' When this forks bear right, across fields, to join a tarmac road. Turn left. An elegant footbridge leads across the Derwent into the hamlet of Portinscale. The derivation of Portinscale is 'harlot's hut'. Those sex-mad German miners again?

Continue up the road, past the Derwentwater Hotel, to a T-junction. Bear left along the road, passing the Derwentwater Boat Club. Shortly after passing the Derwent Bank Guest House, a lane end on your left signposted 'Catbells by Nichol End, Lingholme, Hawes End,' and the entrance to 'Fawe Park', a gap in the hedge to your left will be reached signposted 'Footpath to Brandlehow'. Go through the gap and climb through woods before descending to a junction of paths near a wall. Continue alongside the wall to reach the entrance to Lingholme Gardens. Go through the gate to the right of the entrance, signposted 'Footpath to Brandlehow and the Lake'. A woodland path, giving a dramatic view of The Catbells, leads to a gate on the edge of a field. Cross the field to a gate, cross a clapper bridge, and climb through trees to emerge on to a road.

Follow the signs 'Hawes End' and 'Boat Landing'. The tarmac leads down to the dwelling at Hawes End. Pass to the left of this and look for a gate on your left. Go through this and down a field, passing close to the shore of Otterbield Bay, to a gate. Barely breaking the surface of the bay is tiny Otterbield Island, with larger St. Herbert's Isle looming beyond. The latter was the seventh century hermitage of a friend and disciple of the Northumbrian saint, Cuthbert. Otterbield means 'otter's shelter, or den'.

Beyond the gate the path bears left through a swampy gap between woods to emerge on to the shore of Victoria Bay near a landing stage. About a mile of delightful walking follows, the path twisting along the rocky, wooded lakeshore. When the Brandlehow landing stage is passed, a gate leads out of the woods. A huge water wheel once trundled noisily on the shore of Brandlehow Bay, pumping water out of Brandley mine, whose shafts went deep into the stony vitals of the Catbells. Postlethwaite, whose 'Mines and Mining in the English Lakes' is a classic, states that as well as lead and copper, traces of gold were discovered here.

Beyond the gate turn right and climb up old spoil heaps and past a blocked adit to emerge on to a road opposite an old quarry. Cross the road and climb left along a grassy path across the fellside. Look out for a plaque on an outcrop to your right commemorating the writer Hugh Walpole, who lived just below. His major work was a saga about the Herries family – a kind of Lakeland 'Dynasty'. I've only read Book One, 'Rogue Herries'. It features stirring stuff, such as the Jacobite siege of Carlisle and a moonlight swordfight near Styhead, or was it Sprinkling Tarn?

The path narrows alongside a wall before joining a broader path. Turn left down this to a gate signposted 'Permissive footpath leading to Public Footpath to Rosthwaite/Seatoller'. Turn right and follow the path inside the fence shortly to pass above a walled plantation. When the wall turns away, posts mark your path across the open fellside. Continue above or alongside walls and fences to a crossing of a rocky beck near a wall. Turn right, alongside the wall, to a stile in a fence. Cross this and follow a yellow waymarker to pass between a walled plantation (High Close) and a small fenced sewage works. Follow waymarkers down towards a gate but, before reaching it, turn right along a stony path leading to Hollows Farm. Pass through the farmyard and follow the tarmac road beyond shortly to turn right and join your outward route near the 'No Camping, etc.' sign. Retrace your steps through the campsite to the path forking right signposted 'Bridleway – Seatoller/Honister'.

Follow this path up into the impressive ravine dividing Castle Crag and Goat Crag. Now a lovely highway for fellwalkers, the old quarries greening and harmonising into the fellsides above indicate it was once a hive of industry. At the head of the ravine the path swings right to a fork marked by a cairn and a blue arrowed waymarker. Take the left and lower fork down to and across footbridges over Tongue Gill. Beyond it, follow a path climbing gradually across the fellside, above and to the right of a wall, and heading into the gap between partially wooded High Doat and a rocky spur of Dalehead.

Just through the gap, two gates in a wall corner are reached. Go through the left-hand gate and down a cairned path to join a crossing path near a clapper bridge. Turn left then almost immediately right, by a cairn, on to a narrow path down the steepening fellside to emerge on to the Honister Pass road just above Seatoller. Walk down through Seatoller to the car park.

**Walk 12**                                              **8 miles**
                                              **3000 feet of ascent**

# Dalehead via Castle Crag and High Spy

*An unusual Borrowdale approach to fells more frequently climbed as part of the popular Newlands Horseshoe. Castle Crag is one of those splendid minor fells that given a two thousand foot injection of volcanic ash would rank amongst Lakeland's finest. Rising steeply out of the rocky ravine behind Castle Crag is the craggy eastern Goat Crag flank of High Spy. Pocked by old and greening quarries, their*

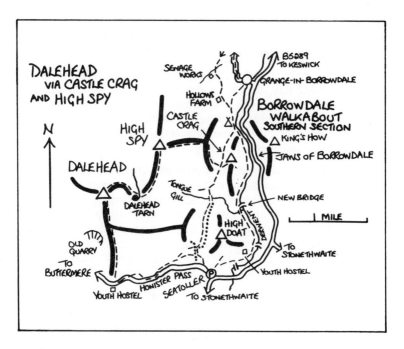

*workshops crumbling on to ledges thick with wild flowers, it offers easy but entertaining scrambling giving a superb outlook over upper Borrowdale.*

*Parking/Start: As for Walk 11.*

FOLLOW the directions given in Walk 11 as far as 'Beyond the gate a path forks left, signposted 'Bridleway – Seatoller/Honister'. Now turn left and climb this path to emerge out of the trees and into the impressive ravine between Castle Crag and Goat Crag. Continue up the ravine, passing below the steep screes of Castle Crag, to where a path forks left near a cairn. Climb this path through a gap in the wall to a stile over a fence. Cross this and turn right to a wall with stiles. Don't cross these but climb left alongside the wall, under some fine pines, on to a path winding steeply up through the tumbled slate hacked out of the summit of the fell to reach the topmost rocks which bear a memorial tablet to Borrowdale men who fell in the Great War.

The rugged incisors of the 'Jaws of Borrowdale', nipping in, restrict the views from Castle Crag. Nevertheless, as you step up on to the summit you are greeted by a fine 'surprise' view northwards of Derwentwater backed by the broad maternal skirts of Skiddaw. Southwards, Glaramara is predominant, a sprawling armchair of a fell with Thornthwaite Fell and Rosthwaite Cam forming bumpy armrests to the uncomfortable seat of Combe Gill, knobbly with drumlins like faulty springs.

There are many Castle 'crags', 'hows', 'heads' and 'rocks' in Lakeland. Invariably, they are isolated rocky hillocks dominating a valley mouth or the foot of a pass. Undoubtedly, their common name springs from a time when they were look-outs or forts defended by primitive earthworks. When standing on the airy crest of Castle Crag it is easy to visualise how effectively it would fulfil either role.

Return the same way back into the ravine. After passing through the gap in the wall look across the ravine for a path slanting right from the main ravine path towards spoil heaps. Cross the ravine path and climb right around a spoil heap to a derelict quarry.Climb up the spoil heap to the right of the quarry/cave. Climb left above this on a barely discernible built-up quarry path which merges into the rocky bed of a beck. When the beck curves right climb over the grassy bank to the left and across the fellside to another derelict quarry.

Note a holly tree growing above the quarry/cave and another holly further right. Now climb up the broad heathery buttress, crowned by a rocky hummock, rising above the right hand holly tree. Keep close to the right edge of the buttress and you will find more rock thrusting through the thick pelt of heather than you might suspect. The final hummock is particularly clean and bubbly rock. Beyond this the fell leans back in broad grassy slopes towards the unseen summit of High Spy. A rocky vertebrae of low outcrops runs westerly up the slope. It's probably the feature marked Lobstone Band on the map. If followed assiduously it continues the easy scrambling virtually onto the well-worn, north-south, path crossing the summit dome. Turn right along this path to the fine cairn crowning High Spy, 2143 feet.
A few feet west of the cairn the ground plunges into the Newlands valley. Across the gulf rises pallid slabbed Hindscarth, with the delectable cones and domes of the Coledale Fells rising beyond. To your left, Dalehead dominates Newlands, with Gable's shapely cone and the lordly Scafells a rugged backcloth.

Now retrace your steps and continue south down the worn path to reach Dalehead Tarn. Cross a beck and pass to the right of the tarn to start the steep climb of Dalehead. Fine views back down the long fell corridor into pastoral Newlands, and close-ups of Dalehead's precipitous northern flank, are a good excuse for 'breathers'.

From Dalehead's handsome summit cairn, at 2473 feet, descend easily south on a well-cairned path, planted with the odd rusting fence stanchion. When a wood and wire fence is met, follow the path alongside to emerge on to the summit of the Honister Pass road opposite the Youth Hostel. Turn left down the road to where the grassy 'old road' forks left. Follow this down to eventually emerge on to the tarmac again. Continue down to where the 'old road', signposted 'Bridleway', forks left again. Follow it across the fellside in a gradual descent. Ignore a 'Bridleway' forking left and follow the 'old road' past a plantation and through a gate. Shortly, after crossing a clapper bridge, turn right by a cairn and follow a narrow path down the steepening fellside to emerge onto the tarmac just above Seatoller. Walk down through Seatoller to the car park.

**Walk 13**

**7 miles**
**3000 feet of ascent**

# The Gable Traverse

*It's sheer whimsy to attach personality to mountains, but mountain climbers are addicted to the habit. Gable, as it is more commonly known to the faithful, is regarded with awe and affection. Rightly so, too. It looks good from all angles, a feature not particularly true of most Lakeland fells. It offers a variety of pleasure and wonderment to climber, scrambler and walker alike. For the fellwalker who enjoys some relatively easy scrambling the route described below is, in my opinion, the most enjoyable way to the top of this much loved fell.*

*Parking/Start: On the verges of the road leading to Seathwaite Farm in Borrowdale. (GR235123).*

WALK into the farmyard and turn right through a metal gate and an archway. Beyond the footbridge over the infant Derwent, turn left through a gate in a wall. The path follows the river past a plantation then gradually climbs right across the flank of Base Brown to enter the rocky ravine of Taylor Gill Force. A rocky scramble of a path leads across the right bank of the ravine and offers a fine view of the waterfall. Above the fall the angle eases and the path follows the right bank of Styhead Gill before merging with the path from Stockley Bridge near a footbridge. Continue up to and past Styhead Tarn, an austere water, its environs often marred by campers' rubbish, but graced by the rugged backcloth of Great End, Scafell Pike and

Lingmell. Nevertheless, I've welcomed its chilly embrace after a hard hot day on the tops. Gable is a disappointment from hereabouts, presenting a uniform slope of scree scabbed with the odd rocky outcrop.

Continue past the tarn to reach the crest of Styhead Pass, crowned by a Mountain Rescue box. This is one of mountain Lakeland's 'Spaghetti Junctions'. Five important paths meet around the box. You have climbed one and to your left (east) a path heads towards distant Esk Hause. The path immediately to your right is the 'tourist', or 'Breast', path climbing north-westerly to Gable top. The path ahead of you shortly swings west to descend across the south flank of Gable to Wasdale Head. The Gable Traverse path departs the Rescue Box area between the 'Breast' and 'Wasdale Head' paths.

Follow it to pass through huge boulders below the quarry-like crag of Kern Knotts. Those interested in Lakeland climbing history should scramble up into the steep greeny corner split by the 'classic' Kern Knotts Crack and Innominate Crack climbs. Beyond the boulders below Kern Knotts the 'traverse' climbs leftwards, passing a seeping spring in a shallow cave, towards the spiky and increasingly impressive rock towers of the Great Napes. Cross the shaly ruddy furrow of Great Hell Gate, which is dominated by the leaning rocks of Tophet Wall, and cross the base of the Great Napes. When the path forks, follow the upper path leading into the slithery bed of Needle Gully. Climb this to where polished holds on the gully's left wall lead on to a collection of fairly spacious ledges known as The Dress Circle, a self-explanatory name for the ringside view it offers of performers, if you're lucky, on the renowned Napes Needle. Scramble leftwards from the Dress Circle. A slab is followed by a climb into a squeeze behind a large rock flake. A short awkward descent beyond leads into Eagles Nest Gully.

Away to your left now is the much photographed Sphinx Rock. (On May 29th, 1953, Everest was climbed for the first time. On the same day, a chilly, damp, blustery one in Lakeland, a friend Derek and I edged nervously up a rock climb on Arrowhead Ridge, above you here. Every anniversary of that triumphal first ascent, Gable sends me a warm memory of a more modest but personal success.) Narrow paths lead below and behind the Sphinx Rock, the lower being the easier. Scramble beyond into the stony shaly bed of Little Hell Gate. Toil up Little Hell Gate to reach the crest of a narrow grassy ridge linking the Great Napes to the main mountain. A more interesting route to the same spot, which avoids Little Hell Gate's shaly grind but

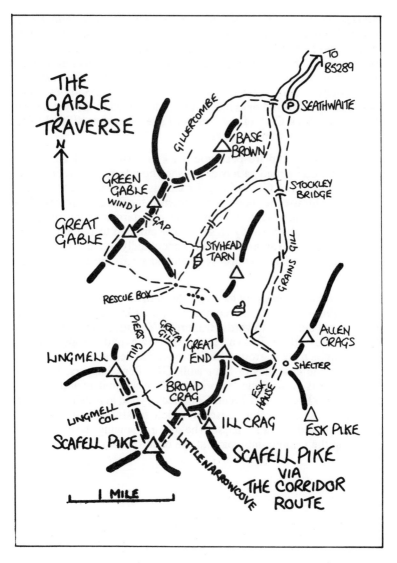

THE GABLE TRAVERSE

TO B5289

SEATHWAITE

GILLERCOMBE

BASE BROWN

GREEN GABLE

WINDY GAP

GREAT GABLE

STOCKLEY BRIDGE

STYHEAD TARN

GRAINS GILL

RESCUE BOX

PIERS GILL

GRETA GILL

GREAT END

ALLEN CRAGS

SHELTER

LINGMELL

BROAD CRAG

ESK HAUSE

LINGMELL COL

SCAFELL PIKE

ILL CRAG

ESK PIKE

LITTLE NARROWCOVE

1 MILE

SCAFELL PIKE VIA THE CORRIDOR ROUTE

involves more scrambling, is to scramble up into the gap behind the rocky hump above and behind the Sphinx Rock then pick a line up rocky grooves, ribs and walls to emerge directly on to the crest of the grassy ridge.

A path leads along the ridge to the base of Westmorland Crag. Climb left along the base of the crag and up its left hand edge. Once

43

above the crag, walk right to the obvious Westmorland Cairn, reputedly built by the brothers Westmorland to mark what they considered to be the finest viewpoint in Lakeland. Given a fine day one wouldn't argue with their choice. A brief climb north-east brings you to the cairn crowning Gable's bouldery dome, 2949 feet. I saw my first mountain sunrise from this spot, aeons ago, yet another reason why I cherish this old bald hill. A tablet dedicated to the war dead of the Fell & Rock Club of the English Lake District is affixed to the north side of the summit rocks.

Placing, without disrespect, your back to the memorial, head north at first along a cairned path over polished boulders, soon veering east to avoid the rim of Gable Crag. From this rim I was once fortunate enough to glimpse the phenomena known as the Brocken Spectre. The path steepens then slants left down on to the narrow saddle of Windy Gap. A short shaly ruddy ridge is now climbed to reach the cairn crowning Green Gable, 2603 feet, undoubtedly the finest viewpoint for Gable Crag, rising in massive splendour across the depths of Stone Cove.

Descend north-easterly to where the path forks, above the head of the hanging valley of Gillercombe, near a rocky hummock. The old fence posts bear left towards Brandreth. You fork right down to the saddle below Base Brown. Here, the main path drops left into Gillercombe to skirt around Base Brown and descend to Seathwaite alongside the cascades of Sour Milk Gill. Peak baggers, however, should climb north-easterly to capture the summit of infrequently visited Base Brown, 2119 feet. Continue beyond in roughly the same line on to an interesting descent which twists around crags and massive boulders, and passes below a 'hanging stone', before rejoining the Gillercombe path at the head of Sour Milk Gill.

**Walk 14**
          **11 miles**
**3200 or 3600 feet of ascent**

# Scafell Pike via the Corridor Route

*Wainwright calls this route 'the finest fellwalk in the Lake District'. Whether one agrees or not with this statement, coming from the master Lakeland guidebook writer it does mean that it is a walk of distinction. It's becoming a bit battered, a fate all fine walks suffer by their very nature, unfortunately. We guidebook writers must accept some responsibility for this. Nevertheless, it still battles through England's roughest and highest ground, and the views are unchanged and memorable. Unlike many popular routes, it is no dull plod and in winter or bad weather conditions requires a certain degree of commitment and capability.*

*Parking/Start: As for Walk 13.*

*Follow the directions given in Walk 13 as far as 'crowned by a Mountain Rescue Box.*

NOW turn left, east, along the path that climbs, ultimately, onto Esk Hause. Just before reaching obvious rocky outcrops on your right a cairn marks the start of a path forking right, through a gap in an old wall. Turn right and follow this path to reach the foot of the rocky ravine of Skew Gill. Cross the gill, climb the far bank, and continue to a fork. Follow the upper (left) fork. The 'Corridor' route slants up a line of natural terraces, passing below the craggy flanks of Great End, Round How and Broad Crag, and above the shadowy rifts of Greta Gill and Piers Gill. Clearly marked by the passing of zillions of boots the path provides a remarkably easy way through some very rough country. When I was a mountain-mad lad it was commonly called the 'Guides Route', presumably because early tourists were led this way by local guides.

As you climb, away to your right Gable, Kirkfell and the further Mosedale Fells bare their rocky chests – a right macho crew these – whilst close at hand the shattered crags of Lingmell plunge into the depths of Piers Gill. In 1883 a climber was injured whilst exploring its depths. Mountain rescue was a matter of self-help in those days. Whilst some of his companions rendered first aid others 'kidnapped' a farm gate to serve as a stretcher, and another found himself galloping down Wasdale on a borrowed horse for the nearest doctor.

Approaching the head of Piers Gill paths fork left, up into the rocky defile below the saddle dividing Broad Crag and Scafell Pike. Ignore these and continue on, passing above the head of Piers Gill towards the Lingmell Col, the saddle between Scafell Pike and Lingmell. Here, a path climbs left up the boulder fields to reach the monster cairn crowning the summit of Scafell Pike, 3206 feet, the roof of England.

(Before leaving the Lingmell Col and climbing to Scafell Pike the energetic peak-bagger should climb right to the summit of Lingmell, 2649 feet. The diversion to climb this comparatively neglected peak is worth the effort for the views it offers, particularly of Great Gable. Gable's south flank, bandoleered with crag, slashed with bloody furrows, draped with scree and scarred with paths, appears to rise at an appalling angle out of a gulf of mountain air. Return to the Lingmell col and climb Scafell Pike as described).

My most vivid memory of Scafell Pike is shivering by its cairn in the early hours of Coronation Day, 1953. We'd climbed the peak in order to see the sun rise in the dawn of a new reign. We found ourselves in thick mist and falling snow – in June! We appeared to have the mountain to ourselves, but the tiny Union Jack fluttering on the cairn – the kind children stick in sand castles on the beach – showed that other daft patriots had passed this way.

Descend north-easterly from the Scafell Pike cairn. Cross the boulder field to the left of a stone shelter to reach a steep rocky ridge leading down on to the narrow saddle below Broad Crag. The crag-lined combe to the right of the saddle is Little Narrowcove, leading to Upper Eskdale. To your left a rocky defile leads down on to the Corridor Route, a useful escape route should conditions warrant it. Otherwise, climb from the saddle on to the bouldery dome of Broad Crag. If the boulders crowning Scafell Pike are man traps then the boulders of Broad Crag are tank traps! The summit rises to the left of the path but all true fellwalkers should make the effort to climb on to it. At 3054 feet it is one of England's handful of three thousand footers and should be treated with due respect, not ignored. Beyond Broad Crag the path dips to a saddle before climbing east then north-easterly across Ill Crag's summit dome. Again, the true summit, which rises to the south-east, is bypassed. I naturally assume that readers of my guidebooks are not prone to such slipshod unethical habits and will make the short climb to the cairn at 3025 feet. They will be justly rewarded by a view of the silvery Esk wending through the verdant swampy reaches of the Great Moss.

Beyond Ill Crag a final bouldery stretch snaps at your ankles before the path bears right down into the grassy hollow of Calf Cove. (The energetic peak-bagger should divert left at this point, across the head of Calf Cove, for the short climb north to 'bag' the summit of Great End, 2984 feet. A circumspect exploration along the north east rim of Great End is rewarding. Deeply bitten into it are the heads of the gullies that provide exciting snow and ice climbs given the right conditions. Dark Sprinkling Tarn is framed between stark gully walls, with Borrowdale unfolding away towards distant Skiddaw. Follow cairns south-east down a stony fellside to emerge on to the grassy saddle of Esk Hause, rejoining the path from Scafell Pike.)

Meanwhile, the less energetic should follow the path down Calf Cove also to arrive on Esk Hause. By a cairn a path forks left, north, descending below the eastern rim of Great End's crags to join the well-worn highway linking Wasdale and Langdale over Esk Hause. Turn left down this path, passing below the gully-riven crags of Great End and above the sanguine banks of Ruddy Gill. A renovated path drops right into the bed of Ruddy Gill just before it twists right. Follow this path, cross the gill, and climb the path up the far bank. It's now simply a matter of following the path down the valley, commonly named Grains Gill, to Stockley Bridge, and beyond to Seathwaite. Grains Gill echoes to the signature tune of mountain Lakeland, a constant susurration of cascading water, both invigorating and restful.